My Truth will set me Free

THINGS BURIED IN THE DARK COMING TO THE LIGHT

CHERRELLE HANEY

My Truth Will Set Me Free: Things Buried in the Dark Coming to the Light
by Cherrelle Haney

ISBN 979-8-218-43658-2

Some Scripture references may be paraphrased versions or illustrative references of the author. Unless otherwise specified, all other references are from the King James Version of the Bible.

Printed in the United States of America

DEDICATION

I dedicate my book to my son, Rajah Haney, who is the love of my life, and the boy who has made me a mother. My auntie/mom, Liza Haney-Nelson. May she rest in heaven. A special dedication to my counselor, Natalie Sanders. God placed her in my life at the right time. I am deeply thankful for her, and may God bless her abundantly.

TABLE OF CONTENTS

Chapter 1:

THE BIRTH

On January 1, 1987, an Angel herself was born. Normally, New Year's Day is a happy and exciting holiday that is celebrated by most folks across the world. However, on this particular day, things were different for Angel or for her mother who had just given birth, bringing her into the world. Young and confused about life and what it had to offer, as a young teenager, Angel's mother had become pregnant at a very young age, which meant that if she couldn't provide for herself already, how would she be able to take care of a child?

Angel's mother, Tara, was the youngest sibling of three. Mary and Charles, being her older siblings, were only teens themselves so they couldn't take care of a newborn as well. Hazel was the grandmother of Tara, which made her great granny to Angel. Hazel was present after Angel's birth; and who would have ever thought that they would hold a special bond.

When Tara and Angel were discharged from the hospital, Tara decided to involve the social services and gave up Angel to a married couple. Although Angel was with this married couple for only a short amount of time, her entire identity was changed, from her name, down to her social security number.

But for some reason, this arrangement did not feel right to great-granny Hazel. She wasted no time in getting her great granddaughter back and decided to take over care for her. So, over the next two to three years, Angel was raised by great-granny Hazel. They weren't the best years, but to Angel's great-granny Hazel, she was her everything. Great-granny Hazel's home was kind of the go-to place when family members and few friends wanted to party sometimes. You see, Angel comes unfortunately from a family background of drugs and alcoholics.

There were good days and sometimes there were bad days of Angel witnessing things that a child should not see at her age. Most days, everyone was too intoxicated to even notice, and this was a regular thing in their environment: loud music, strangers coming and going. Angel didn't have anyone to play with as she was an only child for a while. Great granny didn't play about being potty trained. Most days, Angel would be on the potty all the time, and when she saw her mother, she'd be so happy.

By the age of three, Angel was back with her mother, Tara. Now at this age, Angel was a big sister to her little brother, Legend. Three years later, she gained a sister, Stormy. Each child of Tara's has a different father. Angel never knew of or had ever seen her father, but her siblings' fathers were present in their lives. Angel was the first grandchild, great-grandchild, niece, and pretty much the only child before her siblings came along. Therefore, this made Angel kind of spoiled, and most of the attention she gained was from family members.

Tara had a sister named Mary. Angel was Mary's first niece, and over the years, they grew and became very close. Mary was also Angel's godmother who spoiled her rotten, and Angel adored her one and only auntie. Four years later, Angel was introduced to her cousin Sunshine; over the years, they would grow together and become close. The three siblings and their cousin were very close, especially because they were all close in age as well. Everyone got along for the most part.

Legend, being the only boy, was the protector. Angel's family was quite small, meaning that there weren't many family members at all, and they didn't have very much, but they always had each other. And

Sunshine being the only child, she was always around cousins quite often. With Angel being the oldest, she mostly took charge and bossed everyone else around but not in such a mean way that the other older siblings normally do. But they looked up to her. Sometimes, Angel wished that she had older siblings or siblings around her age because playing with younger kids often got boring.

Legend and Sunshine were crybabies, and once someone cried, everybody got in trouble. As she got older, she enjoyed going to school where she made friends who were at least her age, and it was a chance to get away from her siblings for a while. She wouldn't have to worry much about getting blamed for things that she didn't do.

Chapter 2:

NO ONE HEARD MY CRY

As the years passed, Tara would marry off her youngest child's father, Pyro. Pyro was older than Tara; but at that time, it didn't matter. She longed for a relationship where someone would love her and her children. Plus, she needed a stable father figure in the home. But Tara would learn the hard way about Pyro—he was the opposite of everything she desired.

Growing up in Angel's home was tough. She and her siblings really didn't have much; and when they were able to afford nice things, including food, Pyro would steal it from them and sell it. Although the kids were too young to understand or know anything, they knew that Pyro's behavior was weird a lot of times. He was very mean and abusive towards two of the kids and with their mother. Some days he would be nice; but on other days, if he wasn't yelling, he was cussing, or whooping the kids.

Sometimes, it would be Tara who he would beat up on, and if that wasn't enough, on Pyro's upset days, he would lock everyone in the house, and no one was permitted to leave without his permission.

Angel and her siblings were too young to know what drugs were and the addictions you could get from using them. Pyro was a very manipulative and controlling man. Angel always wondered why he disliked and would abuse her so much; even the other siblings would watch, helplessly wishing that she was big enough to protect them and take away their pain.

Pyro would soon force Tara onto drugs, and soon enough, both of them were addicts. For the most part, Tara kept a job or was gone from home here and there, meaning that Pyro was left alone with the kids. Although Angel was in kindergarten, he would still make her responsible for doing many of the chores around the house.

On a gloomy fall day, a day that Angel would never forget, Pyro called her into his room. He told her to sit still as he began to touch her and make her do things that kids were not supposed to do. She began to cry hysterically, and as she did, he would get upset and threaten to beat her. When he was finished, he would always say to her that no one would believe her and that he would beat her badly if she ever thought to tell anyone.

Though Angel was very young and there were things she didn't always comprehend, she certainly taken the threat posed by Pyro seriously. You see, Angel was a loving, smart, cheerful, and outgoing little girl. Shy, yes, but there was something charming and special about her.

In the neighborhood that her family lived in, there were not many kids her age to play with so a lot of times. She played with her brother and sister; then other times, she played alone, using her imagination, which she was good at doing anyway.

Her Aunt Mary had lived next door with a guy she dated for a while and that made Angel very happy because she could always visit her aunt and cousin because they stayed so close. Aunt Mary would buy Angel cool lunch boxes and prepare her lunches all the time. Between Mary and Angel's mother, Tara, they both made the best lunches for her with delicious goodies every time. Every other day before school, Angel would stop over at Aunt Mary's, and she handed her the lunch box, kissed her, and told her how much she loved her. Then she watched her walk off to school.

Going to school was an escape for Angel, or at least for half of the day. School was somewhere that she could feel safe, protected, and could enjoy being a kid without being yelled at or cussed at. Life wasn't great, but it was simple for Angel. Going and coming from school every day, playing outside or inside the house in their room where there were toys that kids could only dream of having. She and her siblings owned tons of them.

At other times, Angel's family would go over to other families' houses. For instance, Noel's was the favorite, and that was because there were tons of kids of all ages there. A few times, kids would even be mean or bully Angel, but it didn't bother her as she just wanted to fit in and was happy to be included at most times. Though it all seemed good then, going back home was when all the happiness and fun would fade away, and reality would soon set back in.

Most times when the family went out to other people's houses, grown-up parties were happening or small gatherings. The thing about these parties or get-togethers were that it wasn't the average party. There was always loud music playing, people yelling or talking loud, dancing, drinking and smoking – just having a good time. So, most of the time, the kids were free to do whatever they wanted, it wasn't like the adults were paying them any attention anyhow. However, it wasn't a good thing that there was always a kid crying or getting hurt by another kid. Unfortunately, sometimes, Angel would be one of those kids; there were a few cousins who would pick on her and do mean things to her when she came around. Mostly because they knew that she was slightly gullible, but she only wanted to be accepted as the other kids or family members.

Chapter 3:

THE GETAWAY

Going home after family or friend gatherings was sometimes frightening. Tara herself or the kids would never know what kind of mood Pyro was in or what he would do when they returned home. At times, Pyro would be high and without a care in the world, but there was hell to pay when his high would come down. Anything Tara or the kids did the day before, Pyro would beat them the very next day, reminding them that he didn't forget.

It hurt Angel tremendously to see or have to hear her mother being abused and crying. She felt helpless and was sad because there was no one to tell and no one to help them. They were prisoners in their own home. They rarely had visitors over, and when they did, it was freedom for only a few hours. When the company left, it was right back to the basics.

As usual, Tara would leave for work or take care of business. Therefore, that meant for Pyro to be home with the kids, which was always the worst. Pyro would make sure that the siblings stayed in their room, but he'd always order Angel to meet him in the bedroom.

Angel didn't fully understand what was going on or even how to feel. All she did know and understand was that she was in pain, and there was nothing anyone could do because she wasn't able to tell a soul. This cruel and disgusting act went for a while, to be precise, for a few years, but no one ever knew.

One day, though, Angel decided enough was enough, and, to get rid of Pyro, she decided to tell her mother about the situation. She was afraid and nervous, not knowing what to expect or what the consequences would be. Angel was devastated and humiliated when her mother told her that she had made it all up and that she was not to be believed.

As a child, Angel was beyond confused, hurt, and frustrated as to why her own mother would say such a thing. The one and only person that she looked up to as her hero, her safe place – how could this happen? She even went to school, telling her teacher, in hopes that someone would take her seriously and that this nightmare could be over. It wouldn't be until three years later that the people would finally listen.

Angel was in second grade and nothing much at home changed really. In fact, the older she got, it seemed as if she strayed into trouble more. It was the smallest thing just being a kid, she always did a great job in school, and she loved reading and learning, but she was never recognized for it. One night as usual, Pyro was arguing with Tara and things escalated quickly, and he began to physically beat on her. While this was going on, the kids slept in one room together in the two-bedroom apartment they lived in.

At times, Pyro would come in the room where Angel slept and steal her money if he knew she had any. Every bicycle that she or her siblings would get, he stole it and would trade it for drugs. She would try to lie about having anything valuable, but it would only turn into him whooping her.

Startled and awakened out of her sleep by Pyro, Angel was confused about what was going on. Pyro pulled and yanked Angel into his and Tara's bedroom, and then Angel noticed that Tara was crying and that he had beat her up. Afraid and nervous, Angel wondered what was going on and what did any of this had to do with her.

Pyro was high on drugs of course and this night, it would definitely show. Pyro yelled at Angel and told her to sit next to her mother; and out of nowhere, he pulled out what looked to be a large carpenter's knife. He walked up to them both while putting the knife up to Angel's neck saying, "Should I kill both of you and should I go to jail?"

Terrified, screaming, and crying, Tara and Angel looked at each other and held hands. It was then that Pyro would molest and rape them both, making them look while this disgusting act took place. Hysterically crying and being told to shut up and threatened that if she kept crying, she would die that night.

Angel had blacked out. The very next day, Angel was in disbelief about what happened the night before. Once again, Angel and her siblings watched again as Pyro would beat their mother.

But little did everyone know that this would be his last time ever. God must have known that Tara and her children had had enough. Great-granny Hazel stayed on the next street over and somehow, some way, Tara had managed to get out of her house and ran for help while Pyro chased her around, threatening her.

To her surprise, someone had called the police, and they came to her rescue very quickly. Where Angel and her family lived, the neighbors were extremely nosey. Everyone was rushing to them asking all sorts of questions or stood just outside their homes, staring. Pyro was arrested and charged for domestic violence, but little did everyone know, this was just the beginning, an introduction to an entire new world to what was really happening in Angel's home, which no one could ever imagine.

Chapter 4:

DIFFERENT FOSTER HOMES

It wasn't very long before Pyro had his first court hearing. But prior to that, Angel and her mother Tara were asked a lot of questions from all different kinds of strangers (the detectives) who Angel knew nothing about. Most of the time, the people asking her questions either made her nervous or scared to answer or admit.

Angel and her mother went to the courthouse for their appointment, but little did Angel know her life would be turned upside down forever. After being investigated and once again answering many questions, Angel would come out into the lobby, and little did she know that she was seeing her mother for the last time. It seemed as if she was literally in a movie, how could this be, why was this happening to me, to us, Angel thought.

Crying hysterically, hugging her mother so tightly that they had to be separated, Angel was miserable. But all along, Tara wasn't fighting for Angel the same way that Angel had fought for her, and this left Angel beyond devastated. Tara was just standing there with this unbelievable blank stare that Angel would never forget.

Everything happened so fast that none of it made sense or seemed real. No one really sat down and explained to Angel what was going on or what happened. All she knew was that her and her sister Stormy were both taken away from their mother. They were now with strangers, heading to a place where they had no idea who the people were; why were they even going there. The girls had none of their belongings, no toys, no clothes, no pictures or anything – just each other.

Finally, they pulled up to a house that they had never seen before. Scared and confused, they were forced out of the vehicle. Next, they were being told that this was their new home and these were the people that they would live with. So much confusion and fear overwhelmed Angel, but Stormy was too little to know what was taking place.

The next few weeks would be life-changing for the girls. There were two people that lived in the home, an older lady who was the foster mom and a foster son who was maybe in his early preteens. There were many changes happening really fast for Angel and Stormy – a new family and a totally new school that was across the street from where they lived.

This school had a bad reputation. The kids were kind of known for being "ghetto." Most students were labeled, and Angel didn't know one label from another, but what other choice did she have? She also found out that the home she's settled in wasn't far from the home where her mother stayed. Angel thought a lot about running away, but then again, she couldn't just leave.

Sadly, everything Angel thought could never happen to her because of the position she was in, was wrong. Because of her attempt to run away on her way to school one day, Angel was forced to switch schools and was made to be kept under a close eye on her every move.

The foster lady wasn't the nicest, and she was very strict. Angel didn't have any friends and was not let out of the house much. Meanwhile, Andrew, the foster brother did as he pleased. He wasn't too nice either, because he was used to being the only child.

No one knew why, but there was something sneaky about him.

When Andrew was upstairs, he would touch her in places where no one should be touched. Sadly, after a while, Angel took this problem to the foster lady, thinking she could confide in her, but she was sadly mistaken. She was told that she was lying and soon shipped off to another foster home for her and Stormy.

Chapter 5:

LOST + NEED TO BE FOUND

Once again for Angel and Stormy, they were entering the new world, around people that they didn't know. It was the middle of the school year and Angel was in second grade, but this was her third time in the year switching schools. She hated having to start over; she was shy and didn't really talk much unless spoken to.

Meeting the new foster people kind of started off rough, but once everything settled, everyone was introduced to each other and everything was explained better. This time around, the girls were able to live in a two-parent home and with two other older siblings. The foster parents won the girls over and started off great. Angel and Stormy were taken on a shopping trip to get new clothes, pajamas, toys, and shoes, something they'd never really experienced before. To add to it and make the day even better, they went to see a popular movie at the actual movie theater.

Though Angel still missed and thought about her mother, the excitement of receiving new and nice things as well as meeting some of the family (foster) members gave her hope. They actually seemed nice and welcoming.

Finally, the girls were introduced to their new neighborhood, and it was amazing. The people were really nice and had nice big homes. Though Angel and Stormy shared rooms, they didn't mind at all. The owners had two cute dogs, and the best part was that they had a hot tub in the backyard. How cool was that! People in Angel's hometown either couldn't afford or didn't know what hot tubs were. Knowing that these owners had one meant they had money.

The foster parents were nice, and the house even had great food and snacks. At dinner time, everyone sat at the dinner table together as a family, which the girls had never experienced.

Another new experience for Angel was attending a new school. The thing about this school was that there were less African American students than the schools she went to before. In fact, at this school, the majority were White kids. Angel was the only Black student in her class, and some of the White students gave her a hard time in the beginning. Later on, Angel would be sure to put them in their place, but she longed to have Black friends so she wouldn't be judged so often. After a while, though, she just got used to it. She started to wish and think what it would be like being a White person. Soon before she knew it, her vocabulary changed, and she wished for long hair like theirs. Maybe she would make more friends and fit in if she were one of them, she thought. It came to a point where she disliked herself because of not being accepted.

Getting adjusted to the new home and new foster parents was a lot better than the last place that the girls were at, and they started to be at peace with everything, at least until the court trial was forced upon Angel, who testified against Pyro. Angel was horrified as she thought that chapter of her life was done and completely over. Being only an eight-year-old, she had no idea of what was about to take place and whether it would stick with her forever.

The trial lasted an entire week, and, for Angel, this just added on to what she had been through. There were tons of strangers who she didn't recognize; and as for the people who she did know, it was as if they all despised her. She was terrified, and sometimes, she had to vomit because of all the attention and being frightened. Finally, the judge found Pyro guilty on all charges, and he would be sentenced to prison for the next thirty to forty years.

Angel had not understood what was going on, but she did know that prison meant being sent away for a crime that has been committed and that the person would be gone for a long time. She was delighted more so that she wouldn't have to continue to testify in court anymore, and that it was all over. Everything went back to normal after that.

Angel and Stormy could finally settle into their foster home with their new foster family and begin to live happily ever after, right?

Chapter 6:

WHEN ALL HOPE IS GONE

For more than a year since, Angel and Stormy remained at the same foster home; to the girls, this was it. Everything felt so right, so much like home; and even though some of the foster cousins weren't the nicest at times, the girls felt like family. Even though Angel faced some challenges at school because of her race (being different) from other students, it took a moment, but she found confidence within herself.

She would no longer be bullied around; it was time that she showed them who she really was, and Angel delivered just that. Living in this foster home gave Angel and Stormy advantages and experiences they'd never had before when they lived with their mother. Though Angel thought and worried about her mother all the time and always hoped that she would be able to see her again, to be honest, this was actually a good life. Of course, the girls were only kids; they got in trouble as well as other children.

However, the difference was that Angel didn't have to worry about being beaten with a wire hanger, a belt, or a switch from outdoors. Not to mention, being yelled at or cussed out, or being called names.

The love and affection the girls were given was definitely a different experience, a good one. No family is perfect, of course, and still has its ups and downs, and this family was one of them. But it was normal; the great thing was at least the girls didn't have to live in fear of domestic violence, knowing that everything would be okay. Most times when there were arguments, the parents were respectful, not letting the kids see or hear them argue most times.

Little did anyone know the arguments were far from one of the secrets that were being hidden. Regardless of anything or anyone, Angel and Stormy, stuck together. Angel always made sure that she would be around to cover and protect her younger sister because all they had was each other.

Sometimes, having each other wasn't enough protection for Angel, but as long as Stormy did not get harmed or touched, that's all that mattered to Angel. Angel lost everything at a young age or, shall we say, everything was snatched from her quickly. The only thing she had left was her loving sister, and she was like a second mother to her. Stormy looked up and clung to Angel on her every move.

Though they both did not understand it all at the time but later in years, they would very much understand, and everything would make sense. It was then that Angel thought that she was loved, cared for, and finally found a family that she could feel protected and provided for.

All of which made this dark secret involving one of the main people who looked after her, so unexpected, so devastating. No one ever paid attention, no one ever noticed when Angel and the older brother were both missing. What went on? Sometimes, he was bold enough to fondle and touch her; that's how sneaky and manipulative he was.

Once again Angel found herself in a troubled space, another close relative who was to love and protect her only abused and mistreated her yet again. The situation went on for a while without anyone knowing, as terrified as Angel was, she only could hope and pray that the odds would not be against her. But she refused to allow this to happen to her again.

So one day, nervously but calmly, she went to the foster parents to address the situation to them. The next day a big family meeting, which included the older brother, failed to help the situation. To Angel's surprise, he cried forceful fake crocodile tears, he lied and swore on God's name. Angel couldn't believe what was happening right in front of her. No solution was solved that very moment.

The next few days were awkward and uncomfortable for Angel; she was embarrassed and beyond humiliated and felt the foster parents treated her differently. A few weeks passed, and things started to go back to normal; after all the lying and fake tears, the foster brother was back on his mission, and Angel was very much in disbelief. She avoided him with all her might because she did not want to look as if she was the problem. Besides, she still loved where they were living.

Chapter 7:

THE FAMILY

Then, the unimaginable happened to Stormy and Angel. Without warning, without any hesitation, they were moved from the foster home and the foster family that they loved. Heartbroken once again, facing another fresh start, and dreading another school change, Angel felt the weight of uncertainty settle in. But this new family that the girls were placed with were actually no strangers at all. Angel was familiar with these people. Stormy, not so much, because she was quite young, but she played a huge role in why they were placed with this particular family. These people were family to Stormy, not so much of Angel, only by marriage. In order to get Stormy, who they really wanted, the girls came paired up. At least they made sure that they did just that.

Noel's family was one of the families that Tara and Pyro used to take the children over to visit when they wanted to party. The girls loved to go because there were always tons of cousins there to play with. But the difference from visiting to being stuck there was big: at least twelve people were living in the house altogether. This was new for the girls as they'd never been in a house with so many people, always commotion, people going and coming. And the holidays were twice as packed as the regular days, so imagine that.

The relatives in the home were all different ages; some were middle-aged, some teenagers, preteens, younger kids, and a few toddlers. Noel was head of the household, a single parent; the people who lived there were mostly her grandchildren that she had adopted. Others were already grown-up children, those adults too lazy to leave on their own. These folks made the house more intense, as Angel and Stormy would learn.

Angel and Stormy both blended right in along with everyone else. Things were very much different from the foster home; the variety of foods, the house rules, the environment itself, and this was in the hood. Loud music out of cars driving by, people being loud walking in groups, even the kids. Back at the old foster house, the environment was peaceful and quiet. People smiled while they walked past you but still went on about their way. Which worked out in Angel's favor especially in their earlier years there; Angel was mostly teased and picked on because she talked properly and was told that she acted White.

The neighborhood and school she was attending made her quickly learn to switch gears or she would have gotten eaten alive. This environment was very much different than other places the girls had been to. Little did they know this was something that was going to prepare them for the long run.

Noel worked mostly first shift, 6:00 am to 3:30 pm, five or six days each week. So, the older cousins would be in charge. About ten to maybe twelve people lived in this house, and yes, everyone was cousins. There was a brother and sister in every group of the kids who stayed in the home. For instance, Nikki, Tracy, and Rico were all brothers and sisters. Then there's Nina and Mane, though they are leaving the household. They're over just as much as (Lucifer), (Spirit), and Nay.

Uncle Tom and Tank were older uncles who still lived with Noel. Tank would come and go every once in a while, but Uncle Tom literally lived there and wanted to control the environment. He was grumpy and just miserable; nobody cared for his attitude and his wanting to always be in charge of things. So, when the when the cousins weren't around or not at the house, who couldn't wait to be in charge? Yep, you guessed right, and anytime that happened, it was going to be a long dreadful day until Noel showed up to save the day.

After a while adapting and fitting in with the others, everything was working okay. Still, there was a cousin who Angel kind of looked up to and followed around because she was older and cooler, of course. Though Angel didn't really notice much of it because she was always nice and wanted people to accept and like her.

But this cousin, Nina, well you can say she didn't like Angel too much. Nina would be so mean to Angel for no reason at all. She went as far as slamming the trunk door down on Angel's fingers when they were getting groceries, putting her into the dryer, picking on her, and just bullying or beating her up, because she knew that Angel was scared to fight back.

Let's be clear, Angel was not a saint; she had a smart mouth and talked back, but other than that, she didn't mean any harm. And when things like that happened, and being jumped on or beaten up by the other cousins, she didn't have anyone to help back her up, all she had was herself. Sure, sometimes the older cousins or adults would step in, but few of those situations would be for Angel's benefit, and it happened on a regular basis, which she sadly grew accustomed to.

Because Angel was not biological family, she was treated very differently from the way they would treat Stormy. Angel wanted to receive love, acceptance, and just to have a family to fit into. At times, she didn't care; but in her eyes, everyone was accepted and family to her; what did she do so wrong to be treated like the villain?

This was all Pyro's fault. You see, Noel is Pyro's mother, which makes her Stormy's grandmother. Stormy of course is Angel's sister. By Angel being the victim of what happened, certain family members acted a certain way towards her. In reality, she was just a young kid and did not ask for what happened to her, but that wasn't the way some saw the situation. Growing older and growing up in the home, the thing Angel was most grateful for was Noel introducing the Lord to her.

Though most times, everyone hated going, Noel was very much engaged and involved in church. They had different programs for all ages, choir rehearsal was mandatory, evening services, church throughout the week, and even vacation Bible school.

Angel liked church. She enjoyed traveling out of town to visit other churches or even the ones in town, but she didn't like singing in the choir. She got in trouble often for talking during services, but she enjoyed church and learning about God, how to be forgiving, thankful to have a prayer life. See the main thing that made Angel was that her heart was already pure. She was kind, generous, loving, comforting, and would give you her last. But still having a good heart, she only prayed to be treated better someday and hoped that what she did would soon pay off.

As she got older, her love for church would soon die off because the household was forced into going so much. Seeing at times that the older teenagers didn't have to go also made the rest of the household want to rebel as well. Noel had a routine when she got up and got ready for church, and everyone in the home was aware of it. Either they would play sick, stall, or take too long to get dressed in hopes that Noel would be pissed and take off without them. Or they would fake oversleep as if they wouldn't hear her calling them. And if any of those worked then great, but you'd better be out the house before Noel got back from church, because it sure was going to be consequences and repercussions.

Chapter 8:

THE STRUGGLE

Besides missing church here and there, Angel had to deal with other issues. She was a preteen, still slick-talking with the smart mouth, not knowing when or how to stop. She was tall and mature for her age – big breasted, which made her look a little older, so of course, it drew attention.

But she was attractive in the face too, and people liked her smile, which she ultimately hated. One main noticeable thing about her – her full-sized lips – caused her to be tortured by family and kids who called her all kinds of mean nicknames, but she usually just sucked it up. One day, her teacher overheard a student teasing her and comforted her by telling her that one day, she would be famous, and everyone would want lips just like hers. Little did that teacher know, she definitely was right. Angel had low self-esteem mainly from being criticized, making her feel as if she wasn't good enough. She truly suffered from mental abuse at a young age.

Balancing school to be cool and fit in and to keep decent grades was one thing, but going home and having to deal with certain situations sometimes, especially when Noel wasn't home, was the worst. When the house was full, whether it was with visitors or just people who stayed there, it made Angel feel protected. But on the days that it was just her and Stormy, a few cousins and Uncle Tom, the main problem maker, then it was going to be a bad day. Uncle Tom was Noel's oldest son, the son who was on drugs who had no kids, but who needed to boss and tell everybody else what to do. He was a thief and woman beater, heck most of Noel's sons were, sad to say. He always wanted to be in charge, wanted to run everything, and had to have the last say.

He just sat around the house mostly eating everything, watching what everybody did and what everyone would bring in so maybe he could take it, and go sell it one day. What he loves to do mostly was to yell and put his hands on those who couldn't fight back, those who were helpless, those who were like Angel. He didn't like Angel; he picked on her every chance he could, and she learned to just stay away from him. Noel couldn't always come to her rescue when he would try to put his hands on her, but one day, she would learn to defend herself and hit back, and enough was enough.

The times when Uncle Tom wasn't there and would be gone for long periods of time, everyone was relieved, and it was as if they could really live without a care in the world and didn't have to tiptoe around or anything. But when he was back, it was as though a gray appeared all over again and life was gloomy. That was only one of many phases that Angel was forced to face through her childhood, one of the many family members who didn't like her. Remember, Angel didn't have a heart like others, so though she would get mistreated, it never dawned on her they hated her until years later.

She suffered a lot throughout her younger years up until her preteen years. Little did anyone know or care enough to defend her. Angel felt left out, or counted out, and most times she was. On top of that, she had cousins who were in competition or secretly jealous because they were used to getting all the attention. But there were so many people in the household that Angel was overshadowed compared to the others.

There was one cousin close to her age whom she grew close to, and whenever she'd visit, they would hang out a lot. At first, Spirit and Nina hung out a lot and were close, but it changed over the years. Spirit would switch between hanging out with Angel, but she liked Spirit, and they ended up being cool.

She was popular in school, everyone liked her, and she and Angel just clicked really well for some reason. Spirit always invited Angel to hang out with Spirit's friends and to go places – not like Nina who was just rude or mean. She never allowed Angel to really hang out with her, there was a gap in the age difference and maybe once every blue moon but not much.

By the time Angel reached seventh grade, she was well-known, mainly for her looks, as many elementary boys had crushes on her. Her family's reputation and well-known name also contributed, which she didn't mind and came to acknowledge at the time. Junior high school was another level; you had to be even more popular, and dress even more in the latest fashion. Angel's sixth grade year is when she started wearing name-brand gear and was known for rocking the latest Jordans. Angel was able to slowly link up with a few friends from elementary, plus she had Spirit there, and they made Angel more comfortable and helped her fit in just a tad bit more.

Now junior high was much better than elementary school. Sure it had its pros and cons, but it was just way better. Maybe it was the fact of being able to switch different classes throughout the day and see your crush or cute boys, but it was cool just to post up in the hallway with your click and be noticed. Starting off wasn't so bad; Angel was able to keep up with her classes and felt great. However, soon enough, her focus would shift in another direction. A direction that she didn't see coming.

Tara was back in Angel and Stormy's life. They were reunited when Angel was in the fourth grade. It had its up and down moments to where Tara would allow for the girls to come over and visit, but in lots of other days, she wouldn't even answer or open the door for them. Angel was confused a lot of times and saddened because she couldn't understand why Tara would treat them like this. When they were allowed over, Tara always took them school shopping and spent time with them. They loved going to the grocery store because they were able to pick out anything they wanted. Plus, her house was full of snacks, which was the total opposite of Noel's. It was more freedom and being engaged with them, which was longed for. But when it was time to leave and go home, the girls hated doing so. As they got older, they were able to stay over at Tara's for long periods of time.

Before, Angel and Tara would get into serious arguments and fights. Yes, Angel grew up having to literally fistfight her own mother, who called her 'bitch' and other disrespectful things. Angel didn't enjoy these things. As a matter of fact, it hurt her any time they would get into it, and that meant she would have to be distant from seeing her mother for a while. Sadly, it became a pattern of dysfunction – Angel and Tara not getting along. She longed for her mother's affection and love, even respected her highly, but it was never enough, and unfortunately, Tara didn't have those motherly qualities.

Chapter 9: SURVIVOR

Angel had experienced so much at such a young age, and she was barely a teenager. The dysfunction that she had to live and deal with became normal to her. She didn't know the difference. Tara's side of the family disliked Noel's side of the family, which was very understandable, but with no one getting along or liking each other, nobody ever thought how this made Angel feel. Tara was her mother, but she was adopted by Noel; Angel always wanted to keep the peace so she just tried to please both women, which would only backfire at times. And because she had such a big and loving heart, she forgave Pyro; and when he would call from prison, she would talk to him at times, but it was mostly to please and make Noel and the family happy.

That was just it – Angel was a people pleaser, but she had suffered so much abuse mentally and physically that she didn't know any better. She was stuck in the middle and wanted everyone to get along.

Among other issues that Angel was dealing with, there was a way bigger and deeper issue at hand that no one in the family would ever think about that was taking place. Even if Angel wanted to speak up to tell someone, once again what if no one believed her, and the outcome would be terrible in a situation such as this. A relative, yes once again another relative, maybe four years older than Angel, acted as if he couldn't stand Angel. Around other family members, he would say mean things, tease her, or act as if her very presence even bothered him when they were around each other.

In all reality, he liked her and had a thing for her; he treated her so badly that she really thought he hated her. This was beyond dysfunctional, and the fact Angel looked to him as being family was even more disturbing to her. Sadly, her virginity was taken without her consent before she started junior high school.

As time went by, Angel caught the eye of a boy at her school. He was no more than a grade ahead of her. She would see him around here and there, and they would flirt with each other, and she began to like him. He always dressed nicely and wore name brand shoes and seemed to have had a nice upbringing – at least better than hers. Soon enough, they got acquainted and exchanged phone numbers. Most people wrote their numbers on scrap paper or such, but this guy, Zion, wrote his number on a five-dollar bill, which made everybody go crazy. Most teens didn't do that, let alone they barely had enough cash to buy lunch. So yes, this was a big deal.

Though this was Angel's first official crush, growing up, the family had already labeled her as fast and boy crazy to the extent that she would get pregnant at a young age. Okay, yes Angel did like boys, but their labeling her like that when most of the family members were up to no good themselves, well, that was hardly fair.

Soon enough, Angel found herself in a relationship with her boy crush. Being in seventh grade with a serious relationship was slightly too fast, but when you like someone, you like them, and no one could do anything about it. They would talk on the phone for hours to the point to where other family members wanted to use the phone, so there was always an argument.

Once Angel and Zion were more serious, they introduced one another to their parents. Now Noel and Tara were good on meeting Zion, but for some reason, Zion's mom and granny weren't too fond of Angel, at least not at first. Zion was good to Angel; he'd shower her with gifts here and there, and they were inseparable in school. Literally, you wouldn't see one without the other so much that they really became a couple that people envied.

She spoiled and adored him, and what really was cool was that, with permission, he'd drive her around and take Angel where she wanted to go; not even boys his age or older would do that. They spent more and more time together, and most times Angel was over at Zion's house or just out and about.

Angel was beyond comfortable with Zion and felt like she could tell him everything; they were best friends. He was the first person that she would talk to about her secret past, about being raped, molested by Pyro, and that the family she was living with wasn't a blood relative. To Angel's surprise, that didn't scare or run Zion off; it only brought them closer. The sad part was that Angel was withholding a dark secret about her being taken advantage of, so she really couldn't lose her virginity to Zion.

Speaking of that family member, he would be jealous and felt the need to act out in private all because he felt as if Angel belonged to him secretly. When everyone was asleep or gone, he would sneak into Angel and Stormy's room and wake her to come to his room so that he could do things to her. To Angel's surprise, it was unbelievable that so many people lived in the house, but they never got caught, not once.

Angel was forced to endure everything that was happening to her because of the circumstances. Besides, who would believe her? Who would come to her rescue and save her, what would the consequences be? She was blessed to have Zion around. He would become her getaway and her safe place. Being with him took most of her worries and pain away for the most part.

But when she had to return home, it was more about survival mode. Surviving criticism that was always thrown at her, surviving arguments or fights because she chose to stand up for herself, survival just to even fit in and to be accepted still. As Angel got older, she would live back and forth between Tara's home and Noel's. There was more freedom at her mother's, and Tara took on a liking for Zion who would come over and chill with the family. Angel's brother and sister liked him as well. Angel was uncomfortable with having him over at Noel's, people being judgmental, or not being as welcoming as they were to other family members' boyfriends.

Chapter 10:

MY GREATEST ESCAPE

Angel and Zion's relationship was far from perfect. After being together for over a year, there were some issues about infidelities. Zion was a liar about such things, so they argued a lot and would break up to make up. Before long, this became a bad pattern for them, though the break ups wouldn't last long. Angel became distracted, she was skipping classes, her grades had become horrible, and she had a poor attitude towards a few of her teachers who would kick her out of class and send her to detention.

She would get in trouble with Noel, but it happened so often that Noel wouldn't notice or care. Angel did whatever she wanted to do most times. She would get a punishment here and there, but that didn't last very long. She stopped going to church, as she figured that none of the older cousins were going, so why should she? Which was very much true.

It got to the point that all Angel cared about was her relationship with Zion. She missed out on most of her teenage years of doing things with her siblings and mother because she was very much tied down, but who could blame her? Zion was her great escape; she was happy and would forget about the negative things that she was going through while being at home. She felt free and nothing else mattered. Having a boyfriend who could drive and had access to his mom's or grandma's car at all times was super.

Though they weren't very close, Zion's mom and stepdad would be good to Angel. Angel and Zion made it very clear that they were meant to be together, and they didn't care if anyone liked it or not. As the two became more deeply involved with one another, that's when the jealousy of other females towards Angel began more, as well as males towards Zion. Angel would lose focus on her main priority, which was school.

She had fallen behind so much that a lot of time, she was ordered to stay after school, or she would have to attend Saturday school, which everyone hated. But what made it cool was that Zion would attend Saturday school as well just because Angel had to do so.

Honestly, this did Angel no good since Zion was her distraction so little to no schoolwork would be completed. She really would buckle down when she was told that she had to attend summer school or fail the seventh grade.

As much as it pained her to have to do so, she attended summer school. After all, it was her own failure that got her into the situation anyway. Summer school wasn't as bad as Angel thought it would be, but still, having to wake up early when she could've slept in late would've been much better. After a month or two, it was finally over, and she was glad. She was happy that she tackled a goal that some people didn't think she could do.

People in the family would always find something mean to say or try to put Angel down. And it worked; Angel didn't know her worth; she was misguided but still had a good head on her shoulders. She was a bit gullible, and that's when people would take advantage. Kindness was absolutely mistaken for weakness most times.

Angel wasn't the type of girl who smiled all the time; she really only smiled when she laughed, or you'd have to be a special person to have her to smile. She was mostly known to have a mean mug on her face, known as "The Bitch Resting Face." Angel would get annoyed when people told or asked her to smile; people would say she had an attitude problem or think that she was mad all of the time. No, this was just how she looked, plus on the other side living the life she had lived, she didn't have much to always smile about. Not to get it twisted. Angel was grateful for everything because she knew what it felt like to have less, and she was very grateful that Noel introduced her to the Lord growing up in church.

People only knew what they could see on the outside, but not knowing the truth and what Angel had been through, they had no idea what she was going through on the inside. She would confide in Zion and tell him what was going on and what she endured during his childhood, but he didn't really understand. Most of the things that happened to Angel, she would block out and put it behind her to move forward. She made friends with girls who lived close by, and Angel told them her dark secret, and though it pained them regardless, there was nothing anyone could do about it.

Another year, but a higher grade. Angel was hoping to get herself together being an eighth grader, but she still didn't take school as seriously as she should have. She had the right idea, but was in the wrong crowd. Being pretty, dressing nicely, having name brand items, having a handsome boyfriend, and being popular will get you envied fast. Most females wanted what Angel had, or they simply just wanted to be her.

Chapter 11:

TOUGH TIMES

Angel was mature for her age but was the typical teenager. Having a boyfriend, going through stuff at home, having mood swings and school made her try to balance everything out. With really no guidance from anyone, she was pretty much left on her own to figure things out. A house full of people, but no one to care enough to lead the way.

When Zion and Angel would break up, which happened 100 times, Angel would confide in Spirit because they were close enough or she would hang out with her friend down the street. But those were the roughest times. Because Zion and Angel were best friends, it tore Angel up when they would break up for days or weeks, and she felt alone, had attitudes, and stressed out.

Zion was out dealing with other females to get attention, and this made Angel act out sometimes in class. Back at Tara's house, they would argue or she would get into fights with her siblings. She needed to do better controlling herself and trying not to allow her hurt or anger get the best of her. Zion and Angel broke up so often that it was to be expected at times. For Angel, this was unhealthy and toxic.

The years passed by, and Angel was brought up and raised by Noel. Every now and then, Noel would get calls from Pyro, the man who molested her and threatened to kill her and Tara. To show how forgiving and how big Angel's heart was, sometimes, he would ask to speak to her. She often declined, but she wanted to make Noel and the rest of the family happy. Think about that, nobody cared enough to ask Angel how she really felt deep down inside. Truthfully, she was kind of forced into this situation; if she didn't talk to Pyro, the family would feel away. On the other side, Angel couldn't dare let her mother Tara find out unless the little relationship that they did have would absolutely be none.

Angel needed to be accepted by her mother as well as the family she lived with. So, she kept it to herself about speaking to Pyro; she wanted to please both Noel and her mother. That was Angel's problem since she was little. She was a people pleaser; she hated confrontation and always wanted to see other people happy even if it was at her own expense. Most people would say she was brave, some said she was crazy, and they would never in life be able to speak to a person who did such cruel things as Pyro did. But not everyone has the type of strength that Angel has or the kind of heart.

That was another thing about Angel – she always did things with pure intentions whether it would get her in trouble or not; she did things from her heart. She never had a motive and was never jealous or envied anyone. That's why when people would act this way with her, she didn't understand why. It would hurt her feelings because all she wanted was people to like her and to be accepted.

Life was hard enough for her already, given what she went through as a child, and still things were happening to her. Silently alone, there would be times that she would cry to herself, questioning her life, praying and hoping that it would get better. That year in school, Angel would be athletic and play on the girls' basketball team.

People didn't know, but she had a passion for basketball. When she was younger, there was a park near her home where she would go often and shoot hoops with a few male friends who helped her out on her skills. There were a few times when Tara, Stormy, and their brother, Legend, would attend Angel's basketball game. Angel took basketball seriously, she even hoped one day to be in the WNBA. She even tried out for volleyball and tennis, but not many Black girls did that, so it was awkward.

After all, Angel didn't get good grades consistently enough for her to take sports seriously. Maybe if she had someone who helped to hold her accountable, she definitely would have progressed differently. At home, she felt as if she had to compete with a few others in the house; Noel always gave praise to certain individuals, and Angel never really seemed to be one of those people. Hell, a lot of times, Angel felt left out or invisible.

The only time she would get attention was when she got into arguments with her so-called aunts or when someone had something smart to say. Going over to Tara's or going to Zion's house helped a lot. She would go over to her Auntie Mary's house to see her younger cousin Sunshine often, too. The only problem was that Auntie Mary lost touch when Angel and Stormy were forced to different foster homes, but when the girls moved with Noel, they were reconnected.

Angel loved her Auntie Mary, but she just hated the fact that she was an alcoholic. Angel and Sunshine got a kick out of Auntie Mary being drunk; she would do silly things, be stuttering or cussing people out which was hilarious at times. Then there were times Angel felt bad to see her in such a bad way. But when Angel, Legend, Stormy, and Sunshine all got together, it was nothing but silliness and laughs all around.

Legend had a quick temper and was quick to fight anybody, so everyone had to be cautious when he was around and not to piss him off. Legend was from the streets like his dad. He was known for his temper and getting into trouble, so people knew not to cross him; he also was very protective of his older sister, Angel.

Legend and Angel would fight because of his uncontrolled temper, but it never made them hate each other. Sometimes, he could be the annoying little brother when her friends came around, but Angel would put him in his place. As he got older, he got into more trouble, and the family would see him less; he'd spend a lot of his time in juvenile jail. His sisters missed him tremendously, but this became his habit.

Because Legend spent so much time away, it started to affect his relationship with Angel. Being the oldest sibling, Angel tried her best to set a good example for her brother and sister. How could she do so when she was never taught or guided herself? Everything she learned was from her own experience. Angel made herself a promise at a young age: she would always give her siblings and future children the love and affection that was missing in her life, and that she would be the opposite of her mother. Her plan was to break every generational curse.

Chapter 12:
THE CHALLENGE

The end of the school year was approaching soon enough, and Angel once again was trying to make up for lost time. As usual, her grades were low; it seemed as though she stayed in detention. From the look of things, she didn't stand a chance of passing the eighth grade if she didn't get her attitude and grades together. The family doubted her, while teachers, even the principal, seemed to give up on her. Family members swore she'd be pregnant before anybody, before graduation. Yes, she and Zion were still together.

It was pretty much Angel versus everyone else. She didn't have a plan, but she wanted so badly to prove everybody wrong who thought negatively of her. So, she challenged herself on not getting pregnant at an early age like her mother did with her, and she did what she had to do in school so that she could get promoted to the next grade.

Not only was she about to become a ninth grader, but her generation would be the first eighth graders to be promoted to high school. This was a huge deal, and Angel had to make sure that she could be a part of this. Zion was encouraging to Angel; he also was being promoted, but to the tenth grade. Angel tried hard not to let her personal issues get the best of her. She had to motivate and encourage herself to push past anything that could hinder her. Surrounded by so-called family, but no one to support her. On the other hand, attending high school was a big deal. Was Angel ready to make that transition?

At least once, her favorite cousin, Spirit, would attend the same school, but it would be Spirit's last year at school since she was a senior. They had a clique of females and had made a name for themselves. Angel was happy to be friends with those that she met through her cousin, although she was the youngest. With her being mature, people couldn't tell the difference.

Junior high had its pros and cons. She had some growing up to do very much mentally as well. Most of her female cousins that lived in the home already attended high school and graduated. It would've helped if they had talked or guided Angel to what or how life was about to be like in high school and how more serious you have to be about your grades.

Her mother was no help or could probably even care less; Tara didn't have any goals nor was she taught anything about having goals, boundaries, achievements, just how accomplishing things could better your life and self-esteem. That was one of the many things Angel longed for, to sit and have those one-on-one motherly talks, and to bond through them. She attempted a few times with Noel, but it didn't really work; she still felt like she was looked over, and things she did accomplish were pretty much overlooked or were not good enough.

Being the oldest, Angel always wanted an older sister of her own, someone who was wise and who could pass their knowledge on to her so that she wouldn't make certain mistakes in life. Regardless of not having someone around or to look up to, her goals were to be a positive role model and example for Stormy and Sunshine. Not to leave out Legend or anything, but it was a little more complicated him being a boy and all. Without her siblings knowing it, Angel tried her best at protecting them, and if they needed her, she always looked out for them.

She was going through so much mentally, but her family loyalty and persistence never wavered. Angel just knew with every challenge that she faced, everything would work out in her favor. Angel hated her upbringing – no one to really guide, motivate, or encourage her. It was pretty much whatever life threw at her, and she always would have to go through the worst just to figure it all out. It was a challenge just to come home from school most days – having to worry or dodge questions, worrying if she was going to be yelled at, wondering whether she would have to get into any arguments or be bullied around the house or picked on because of someone else.

Sadly, these were the things that happened often and that ran through Angel's mind constantly. She used to like going a few houses down from hers when she came from school. One of her close friends stayed nearby, and they would chill for hours or just walk around the neighborhood, it made her feel relieved. Angel was cool with her friend's family because she was around so much. Every now and then, her home girl had a boy cousin that would come over every once in a while, because he was interested in Angel.

Angel had met him maybe over a year ago and the two became very interested in one another, but they lost touch for a short time, and that's when Angel met Zion, and the two of them began dating. It was too late for him, and they remained good friends but that would be all. Yeah, they would flirt a bit, but Angel was taken and always remained faithful to Zion. They lived two different lifestyles, and Angel didn't let that bother her, but she still secretly liked him.

The good thing about Zion, which Angel really appreciated, was that he never judged her or her family. Zion's family lived in a nice house and drove nice cars, and he came from having money. Angel's family, especially her mother's side, didn't really have a lot of money or nice things. Sometimes, she was even embarrassed of certain family members because of their drug or alcohol habits.

Zion truly loved Angel for who she was and not for what she had or didn't have, that alone was a blessing to her. The main issue at most times was Angel's attitude problem. Sometimes, she could be mean to Zion; there were times, of course, where he deserved it. It was so familiar to Angel where a lot of times, she didn't notice that she had one. But the environment she was in caused her attitude. She was misjudged and criticized.

Angel dealing with her childhood and other traumas added to the already existing ones and put her in a bad space. She was left to deal with everything on her own, and she was made to accept things and move on with life. All the dysfunctional things became normal to the point she taught herself to question, 'What is normal?' 'Chin up, and keep it moving.' is what she planted inside of her head, and throughout the years, that's just what she did. In school, Angel would challenge herself. She would do this by telling herself, okay, this week I'll get good grades or turn my failing grade into a passing grade. Yeah, it worked for a moment, but she would always find herself distracted once again or trying to prove a point which got her in trouble.

The problem was Angel didn't take things seriously until it was too late (school). Most times, she would talk her way out of situations, but it would often backfire. She was known for a smart mouth and labeled for her bad attitude with her teachers. Soon enough, if she wanted to pass on to the next grade to attend high school, she was going to have to change that and work harder on her grades because the end of the year was approaching quickly, and she was almost out of time to make the change to get herself together.

Chapter 13:

NO GUIDANCE

Well, believe it or not, Angel buckled down and did what she needed to do to pass the eighth grade; she could be promoted to the next grade. The big day FINALLY happened for her, she had a point to prove, and she proved it to those who doubted her. Was it easy to do? No. It took a lot of time to sacrifice something that she didn't know about at that time but later in life would find out.

She had to push herself and be her own motivation with little to no support. Was it hard? Yes. She hated getting up early on days that there was no school, but she still had to tackle some schoolwork. Did she want to say, forget it, or give up? Yes, but she was determined to press forward to show that she wasn't a failure, that she wouldn't come this far and work too hard just to give up, be laughed at, talked about negatively, or put down.

Walking across that stage at junior high graduation was one of the happiest days for Angel. Being able to accomplish something on her mother's side that no one was able to do meant a lot to her. Tara didn't attend, which saddened her, but with a few others who showed up, and with Zion there to fully support her, it made her not think too much about it.

As exciting as this was for Angel, little did she know that high school was like a whole different world. No one had sat down with her to prep her or give her a head start on the things she was going to experience or the dos and don'ts; she would have to work kind of blindsided to this new experience that she definitely was not ready for.

But until school started back up, she would enjoy her summer break, which she spent mostly with Zion. She missed time with her siblings because of her relationship, but Angel found she was too mature to take part in some of the activities that they did. The time she and her siblings and Tara spent together could have developed a closer relationship. But no one had family meetings, family discussions, or sit downs.

At times, when Angel was over at Tara's and they all had small talk, it mostly ended up in arguments or violence because of Legend's behavior; his temper was out of control and no one was really able to calm him down. Tara or Noel never had the female version of the conversation about the birds and bees, nor the important discussion when you start your period. Not even a sex conversation; Angel pretty much was thrown out there to fend for herself and learn on the way.

What upset her the most was her mother's way of thinking; she would say, "Well, my mom didn't do this or do that for me. So, neither do I need to teach or say it to you just because it was not taught to me." And because she was used to Tara saying these types of things so often, she promised herself to be the opposite of what her mother was to her; when she would have children of her own, she was going to be the opposite of how Tara treated her. The nurturing and loving part that was inside of Angel were things she got from her Auntie Mary. Mary was the opposite of Tara; she was very kind, genuine, and loving, plus she always showed it and acted on it.

Mary instilled in Angel that she loved her and always showed affection, something that Noel and Tara barely showed. At times, Auntie Mary showed her affection too much to Angel, who would be embarrassed, but she knew how Mary meant no harm. She was an alcoholic so she would be drunk most times, and Angel hated that for her, and that's where the embarrassed part would come from. But she loved her auntie with all her heart, plus Mary was pretty much her second mom, and since her cousin Sunshine, was Mary's only child, Angel took her in as her loving second sister. It wasn't a thought now because Angel was experiencing and figuring out life herself, but being the oldest sibling was tough and would be something she would have to navigate through.

Until then, she would just have to ride the rollercoaster of life's ups and downs that were thrown at her. One thing she promised herself was that no matter what, she would not allow life to overwhelm her. She was so embarrassed by family members being alcoholic and using drugs, she vowed never to allow herself to become a victim of those things, no matter how harsh life treated her.

She wanted to be that family member who could be able to look back over her life and say to herself with a smile, "I beat the odds of everything that happened to me, and I did it soberly." Angel never had anyone growing up telling her what happens if you use drugs or drink alcohol. Luckily for her, she was smart enough to know there were some things she didn't want to do. Thankfully, the friends that she hung around weren't into those type of things as well.

Entering high school, she wasn't the best dressed, but she was always well dressed. High school was another level. Not only do you have to be best dressed, but your name brand clothing is what really got you noticed or made you popular. Angel wasn't too worried about being popular because she was already well-known.

Chapter 14: IDENTITY

In the first month or so, high school was overwhelming. The school was huge compared to Angel's junior high school, and there were more classes added to Angel's schedule. The school literally had three floors, not to mention all of the students who attended; if you had a gym class, you had to walk pretty much down the street because it was another building that was not in the school, so just imagine having gym class in the wintertime.

At first, Angel would get lost trying to learn her way around the school, and she would be late, which was embarrassing. Another thing about this high school was that there were three to four principals. Each grade had its own assigned principal, unlike junior high where there was the vice principal and then the other principal. Another scary thing for Angel was that she was used to just mainly having only her grade in mostly all the classes she attended, but NOT in high school. It was a mixture of every grade and all types of different people in all her classes.

More classes meant a lot more school or homework, which started out as her priority but then slowly she began to lose focus. Because everyone knew that Zion and Angel were a good-looking couple, people started to test their relationship. Though a few things happened in the past, infidelity on both sides but mainly Zion's, Angel continued to forgive him and stayed with him. Girls started to notice him more, and because his family was known to have money, females couldn't wait to try to see where they could fit in.

Because of this, Angel started to become distracted and started to skip classes, which was lame. She would hide out in the girl's bathroom mainly, the auditorium, or just walk around the school peeking into other classrooms. Compared to what everyone else was doing when they skipped school, smoking or drinking, even having sex, Angel would occasionally buckle down so she could praise and maybe brag about herself the way she did with certain grandkids. Angel always wanted Noel's acceptance or praise, but sadly, it was like she was invisible most times.

For sure, Angel was a girlie girl, but basketball was always her love. She even went to try out for cheerleading with a friend. Angel did not like being in the spotlight or having all the attention on her. When trying out, she messed up here and there, plus forgot some of the moves. When the list of people who were accepted was posted, even Angel's friend, who did worse than her, found out that she got accepted—but Angel didn't. This devastated her and crushed her pride. She cried all day and even the next day. She was so confused about how she didn't make the cut while her friend did.

Her friend honestly couldn't even afford the uniforms nor was she the cheerleading type. On the other hand, if Angel wanted her grades up, she didn't stand a chance of doing any kind of sport. Sure, she might've got in trouble or yelled at mostly about her grades or being absent, which she mostly denied, but there weren't major consequences.

One of the best and most exciting things about high school were the football and basketball games. Everyone was there. It would always be packed with people dressed to impress, and Angel's clique of friends was older than her, and most of them were cheerleaders. She would come with them, but most times, she would cuddle up and chill with Zion. The basketball games were the same thing, but when her girls weren't cheering, they were all cliqued up with all eyes on them. And they never really watched the games; they were there to be cute and walk around mostly with most girls envious of them but in a nice way.

School dances also were off the hook, but Angel couldn't attend some because she got suspended, thanks to her sassy mouth or for getting into fights. Her school principal couldn't stand her, and they did not get along at all, mainly because she stayed in his office in trouble most times. There was a school dance. Angel got all dressed up and got her hair, nails, and everything done up. She and Zion arrived together right in front of the door; all the principals sat. At times, Angel was able to talk her way out of things, but unfortunately not this one.

The day before the dance, Angel had to be suspended, and the principal told her that because of that, she could not enter. Angel didn't believe what she was hearing. Did he dislike her that much that he had to humiliate her not only in front of her boyfriend, but also those who stood present around her. She was so embarrassed. All she could do was cry. Zion took and dropped her off at her mother's house.

To add to that, Zion didn't make it any better, instead of him maybe staying and comforting her. He left to go back to the dance and even had the nerve to hang out with others after the dance. He didn't even pick Angel up so that she could tag along. Of course, his actions only led to them arguing. The next day, Angel would attend school as if nothing happened. Besides, the school dance must've not been all that great, no one was really talking about it. Still, she promised herself to never again put herself in a situation to miss another dance event. With that, she tried to focus more on her classes. She even buckled down not to skip classes so much. Sooner than later, though, Angel would allow her bad habits to catch up with her. She barely brought homework home and being in high school, there was always homework to be done. Angel was young, and she wanted to always hang out with friends. Not to mention she was in love and had a long-term relationship to manage. No one ever taught her what priorities were, and that, if anything, school was to be first on that list.

With all the attention she was getting, she began to become distracted by all the things that were not much help in improving her grades. For some reason, she thought at the last minute that she could pretty easily get her grades together. She was wrong, and another summer was dedicated to having to do summer school again. Not only was Angel mandated to attend summer school, but she was now kicked out from the high school she attended. Her new school that she was forced to attend had the worst reputation in the city, and Angel pleaded and cried. She even had Noel try to talk to a different principal, but all failed. Angel was expelled, and nobody could do anything about it.

Chapter 15:

THE WAKE-UP CALL

As much as Angel hated summer school, she didn't have much of a choice. It was either attend and make up for certain classes or get held back a grade. There was no possible chance that she would allow for being held back a grade. She had to prove to herself but also to the teachers and principals who didn't think that she could fix everything that she could pass to the next grade.

Nothing about this was easy. Waking up early mornings while everyone else slept in, having to walk to school alone—it was terrible. Unlike regular school, she couldn't just skip classes, and Angel just kept reminding herself that, no matter what, she would be able to move onto the next grade by completing summer school. The great thing about the summer classes was that there wasn't homework. But you had to have your assignments completed and turned in by the end of the day. Not too many, but Angel had maybe three to four classes to complete. It was tough a lot of times. It's hot and nice outside, and you're wondering what your friends are doing.

You're hoping that you're not missing out on anything, so the best thing to do is focus and try not to get distracted. Finally, something happened; the day Angel was waiting half of her summer for. She proved the people who doubted her were all wrong: she passed every class and, though it was a struggle, she had FINISHED. Angel was really proud of herself.

She still wasn't happy about having to attend a different school, which meant new people, new teachers, and having to adapt once again to a different environment. She hated the idea of having to start all over again. Whether it was relationships or schoolwork she couldn't stand the very thought of that. Of course, Zion and her relationship would be put to the test too. She dreaded the thought. Regardless of everything, if she wanted to graduate from school, this is what had to be done. The good thing about this new school was that it started at a much later time, but the downside to it was that the students were out at a much later time than others. Also, because the school was further away for her, she was ordered to ride the school bus. She hated buses and despised anyone who rode them. To make things even worse, she stayed in the hood, and this means she was assigned to certain bus stops, and she would have to walk and be seen by others while waiting, which was beyond humiliating to her. Zion would be a great help by picking her up from school, so that was one relief.

Regardless of everything, Angel now felt as though she was labeled. The school she was attending had bad rumors. Every student that went there was a bad teen, and to make matters even worse, the school really did look like a prison. And just when Angel thought it couldn't get any worse, the same principal who expelled her from the other high school was now following her to this new school. She couldn't stand him; it was like any chance he had he always gave her a hard time. It was a nightmare that became real. She figured, since he gave her a hard time, she'd repay him by doing the same.

She found out it was required for all students to wear uniforms. It would've been okay if maybe they allowed colors of choice, but no, the colors were red and tan. The shirts must be red polos, and pants were to be tan khakis.

Everything about this school was just horrible and embarrassing. Without a choice, Angel had to adapt to this very difficult change. To Angel's surprise, while attending her first week at her new school, she learned that a lot of people from her grade and old high school were sent to this school as well. She became more comfortable and relaxed as she knew almost everybody. There were a few fresh faces, but half of the building, it seemed, was from her neighborhood.

The good thing about this school was that people didn't really hang in big cliques. A few people cliqued up, but it was maybe three or four people. Everyone pretty much did their own thing. There was no competition really because everyone wore uniforms and looked alike. Maybe once a month, they were able to have one dress-down day, and when they did, Angel always dressed to impress.

For the most part, Angel started off the school year right. Her grades were better, and she liked all her teachers. But there was always that one class, boring, uninteresting, and the teacher always made you sleepy.

And math class, for some reason she just couldn't grasp it. She hated math, and it seemed as though it hated her back. When it came to her grades and tests she would fail miserably. One year she passed with a D and then D-, but after that, it seemed to not hold her attention, so then she would skip classes with other people, and they would mainly just walk around the school or hide out in the girls' bathroom.

The difference with this school was that it wasn't as big as the school she left, so it made it more boring. In this school, most of the students did whatever they wanted. Of course, discipline came with it, but these students didn't care and they were wild. It was like watching the Jerry Springer TV show, but with Black teens acting out. Looks like the rumors about this school were true, except the part that all students were labeled as bad. Not everyone was a bad student.

Because the school reputation was that bad, when there were certain events going on, the students wouldn't be allowed to attend. That's what pissed and angered Angel the most, because Zion was at the other school so that made things complicated. When you're used to attending such things, it definitely makes you feel awkward.

This school never hosted any events; it didn't even have afterschool activities for the students.

When she was able to, Angel still attended her old school's events. Lunch time was the pits; there was no cafeteria, actually, and the so-called lunchroom used to be a classroom but held only so many students. There were no options at all to choose from, and this made it really feel like a jail serving crappy food that you had to eat. Most times, she couldn't wait until school let out, because she knew it was something better to eat, or Zion would make sure that she ate a decent meal at McDonald's or Burger King. That was the difference between Noel's and Tara's home. Only on the weekends, Noel would order Pizza Hut for the house, but because so many people stayed there, you would be lucky to get a second slice. Other times, she'd buy Burger King, but Angel didn't really care because it would be all Whoppers ordered from having coupons. She hated Whoppers and was called a picky eater and picked off the toppings, which got her in trouble at times.

Tara was a picky eater, so her kids were as well; they all liked the same things and a lot of times, that helped. Especially when they were much younger, they ate quite a bit of McDonald's, and the kids loved their Happy Meals. There was, indeed, much of a difference between Noel and Tara. Most times, Angel was able to get away with more, because she was back and forth in between houses. It happened mostly when she was in junior high school, dealing with about twenty different personalities in one household and always having to defend herself. Or, being treated differently because they are not really blood related—she would want to live in between homes as well. And not having any structure or discipline at this age, she pretty much did whatever she wanted.

Besides his stupidity of messing with other females, Zion made Angel feel that he was the only one who truly cared, especially keeping her grounded with doing better in school. He didn't have the best grades, but at least they were passing, and he stayed out of trouble compared to Angel. She got along well with all her teachers for the most part, of course. Angel being Angel, she would occasionally say something slick that would get her sent out to the hallway for a slight warning. But it was the dickhead principal of hers from her old school that sent her. She really hated his guts; she couldn't stand the fact that he was there to once again torture her.

Angel had a lot of maturing to do when it came to her attitude. Too often, she was quick tempered and would allow things and people to control her. Lacking self-awareness, it would get her left out of things here and there because of her smart mouth. Depending on who you were, Angel wouldn't just let anybody talk off-key to her regardless of the outcome. Some of the time, her aunts at Noel's house would put their hands on her, but Angel didn't care about the age difference; it was favoritism, and she was the only one who would be targeted.

Chapter 16:
MEMORIES AND MISTAKES

With the end of tenth grade slowly approaching, Angel was passing all of her classes, but the year wasn't exactly glitter and gold for her. Zion completely embarrassed her by dating other people, so there were break-ups here and there. Angel flirted, but it was nothing ever major. At times when they would get back together, whether it was for a holiday or just because, Zion always would bless Angel with the sweetest gifts at her school. He always would bring her lunch, which she loved. This would have made girls jealous and envious. Prom was coming up and though she didn't attend the school where it was being hosted, Zion attended there.

To be precise, this was Angel's third time attending prom. Her boyfriend, who was actually a grade above her, often helped out with events like this one in particular. She loved going to the school dances and proms. She got to get all dressed up, her hair, nails, and feet done. It literally made her feel important and almost like a celebrity. It was great seeing everyone dress up and look nice. Noel always came and made sure that Angel looked her best. For most events, she and Angel would actually go together to look for her dress. Such moments made Angel feel that maybe she and Noel could bond more. Angel had the chance to attend proms and was able to become a sophomore, something that no one on her mother's side was able to do.

The older Angel got, the more she was told by family members that her achievements made Tara jealous. She would be confused and think to herself, "why?" All she ever wanted was to feel loved and accepted by her mother and to make her proud. What did she have that her mom could possibly want? Angel could never accept or wrap her head around what was being said, nor could she believe it. The saddest thing that broke her heart mostly was that her own mother never showed up for Angel's graduations or proms. There were no pictures taken for future memories or any phone calls the following day to chat about her experience. Angel just wanted that mother and daughter relationship, especially because of her situation when she was younger and was physically, sexually, and emotionally abused by Pyro. She thought it would allow them to bond and be closer than ever, but she was wrong. She would always question herself on not being good enough, was she pretty or even smart enough for her mother? Since a younger age, she noticed that her siblings were treated slightly better and had a good relationship with their mother, but not her.

Angel wasn't perfect or innocent and never claimed to be. But she was obedient, respectful, and would always go out of her way and beyond for her mother. She only wanted to make her proud. No matter how hard Angel tried, it would always seem that it was never good enough. Both households that Angel lived in, she always would wonder and question herself. Normally when a child notices that the other siblings are treated better, it makes them have resentment towards each other, but that was the best thing about Angel – she didn't have a jealous bone in her body towards her siblings. She just kept trying and never gave up. Sad, angry, frustrated, misunderstood and all, Angel would still try her hardest.

Not giving up would be one of Angel's many strong qualities. Angel always wanted to get along with people and for everyone to like her; she hated drama, arguments, and people not getting along. It triggered fear inside of her. Though she knew nothing about triggers, or triggering others, she knew how she didn't like the feeling. It would frighten her and put her in a dark place. Her memories of being younger would always play back – her mother getting abused by Pyro, or Angel herself getting whooped or yelled at by him as well.

One main thing about Angel was that she was very prideful. She hated asking anyone for anything; she would rather go without or do it herself. She was always willing to help or give someone her last; that was the type of person she was. For people to overlook her or not be as helpful or nice as she was to them, it really crushed her. Often confused and frustrated, she couldn't understand why people would misuse and take advantage of her. She hated the fact that she was very forgiving, quite gullible, and always giving people the benefit of the doubt.

She got so angry that she started holding onto grudges. Inheriting this skill from Tara's side, Angel initially took advantage of it, but she would later learn that this behavior would ultimately harm her. That was a part of Angel's dark side. If done wrong, she was vengeful as well. Payback was her motto, and she would make you stand on anything you'd done to her.

But her biggest mistake would happen for her that summer after tenth grade. One day, Angel decided to go over to Auntie Mary's house. She visited with her often and loved being around her and Sunshine, her cousin. Though they were a few years apart, Angel didn't care; Sunshine was like a little sister. Of course, the thing about Mary was that she used drugs and was an alcoholic. Angel was Mary's favorite; she spoiled her since her birth. Visiting Mary was like having extra freedom because she was maybe high or drunk from time to time, so her nieces and nephew pretty much did what they wanted to over at her house. She was the cool auntie; never once did Mary ever whoop or even yelled at her nieces and nephew. Auntie Mary was always nice and nurturing.

One other thing about her was that when she was drunk, she loved to dance. Angel and her siblings used to crack up, watching her and mocked her, as well, but it was always a good time. Even though Mary and Tara would get into it because Mary was intoxicated, it would still all end in love. A lot of times, Mary would have strangers over at her house, and they all would get drunk or high all together.

Angel was very protective of her auntie. If anyone disrespected or got out of line with her auntie, Angel would be the one to straighten them out. It was bad enough the people who Mary partied with were using her for her money, the free booze and drugs. It pissed Angel off every time.

So this day, Angel probably took things a little too far; she let it be known that she would never let her auntie or herself be disrespected. Angel had stayed overnight and had seen the guy a few times before at the house. He had a smart mouth, and Angel never paid him much attention; plus, he was somewhat handicapped.

Sunshine and Angel were in another room, minding their business. The guy said something smart to Sunshine, and from there they began to argue. Angel decided to step in and be the peacemaker, but the guy got smart with her, and soon they were arguing. He disrespectfully threw in her face her past of being molested and raped. Before she knew it, she picked up an object and began to beat him with it; she was so out of control that she frightened her auntie. Angel had blacked out.

Soon, she was back at home over at Noel's. A few hours passed by and she was sitting on the stairs in front of the house when the police pulled up. Not thinking anything of it, Angel cooperated with the officer; she thought they were looking for her brother, but of course she wouldn't allow them to know his whereabouts. To her surprise, however, the next thing that happened, she was being handcuffed and put into the back seat of the police car. They took her away without giving anyone the chance to know what was happening. Angel was terrified and shook with fear. She was never in trouble with the law; she only saw it happen with her brother, but never herself.

She thought they'd only take her down to the station and question her, but that's not what went down. To her surprise, Sunshine was handcuffed as well, and they both were on their way to juvenile hall. Confused, scared, and frustrated about what was going on with really no answers, Angel wondered: Who called the cops? Who and why did they give the police her name? Seeing Sunshine calmed Angel's mind a little because she wasn't alone and thinking okay, maybe this will only be an overnight thing, and they'll release us.

But Angel and Sunshine had the biggest shock of their lives – not only were they not released the next day, the two girls were ordered to spend the next forty-five days in juvenile hall. Angel was overwhelmed with grief. The first two days, she wouldn't eat or come out of her room for anything; all she did was cry. Everyday felt like a nightmare happening over and over again.

Chapter 17:
THE HELP

A week passed and there were no words, letters, or even visitations from Tara or Noel. Angel was beyond heartbroken – thoughts of no one caring, who could care less plagued her. All of a sudden, her name was called to go up front. Confused and looking at Sunshine, who was out in the living area watching TV, they both were caught off guard. Angel walked to the front and asked the staff what was going on.

To her astonishment, the staff replied that she had a visitor, and it was her dad. Angel's father was nowhere in the picture, so she knew that couldn't be true, but she didn't respond back out loud. When she saw the visitor come through the door, her mouth dropped, tears filled her eyes, and she just laughed, but not too much. It was Legend and Zion. Zion who was posing to be her father. It was ridiculous because he barely looked even grown, but the fact that he put the effort in and didn't care about the repercussions, it mattered that he came to support Angel. Everyone knew that Angel and Zion were a couple. They had a good laugh and about a fifteen-minute visit before the staff finally caught on. To know that Zion was ready to risk it all just to be able to see and talk to her meant so much to Angel. When the visit was over, she was sad, but she and Sunshine had a good laugh from it.

Still, Sunshine and Angel had to buckle down and serve their time. After a while Angel was able to open up to some of the other females that were there. Sunshine was more outgoing and friendly than Angel, who had to put on a tough image and hold herself and Sunshine down to let everyone know they weren't punks.

A situation happened that involved Sunshine, and Angel was right at her defense and rescue and refused to leave her side. It was only right; all they had was each other and no one else. Because of this situation their bond became stronger, though they both vowed to never talk about the situation that put them into juvenile. They made friends with a few of the females who were there as well.

By the time they all had bonded closely, it was finally time for Angel and Sunshine to be released to go home. And once again, you had some of the girls who were happy to see them off, and then you had the haters mad because they were stuck and not going anywhere. Angel was so relieved to be out that the first place she wanted to go was Burger King.

She was happy, too, that she was still able to enjoy her summer. Of course, word got around about Angel going to juvenile hall, and when asked about it, she was kind of proud she had the image of being tough and not to be messed with. She and Zion reunited and were happy being back together again. One thing about Zion that was important to Angel was that he really supported and looked out for her no matter what. Angel shared her juvenile stories with her sister, Stormy, who eagerly listened to everything that was so unbelievable, even though it had actually happened. Angel was just thankful and surprised that the incident didn't go on her record. With school approaching in the next few months, she just wanted to enjoy the rest of the summer and put the situation behind her and move forward. That summer she spent most of her time at Tara's, even though she was still back and forth between Noel's.

Even though their brother, Legend, was welcome over at Noel's, Angel knew the family felt a certain way about him. Being under one roof over at Tara's with her siblings was a much better feeling when all three of them were together anyway.

Though Legend had a bad temper, everyone had to deal with him carefully, which was kind of hard to do at times. But no matter if they were upset with each other, they all had each other's backs at all times, and Legend didn't play about his sisters at all. When Angel got tired of staying at Tara's, she would go back over to the other home and vice versa. The good thing was that the two homes weren't too far from each other, so she could walk from one house to the other. At other times, Zion would take her to whichever home she desired to be dropped off at. Since maybe the ninth grade, most of the summer she would spend almost all of her nights sneaking into Zion's room. His granny would catch them, but they didn't care; they would just find another or better way the next day. They literally were inseparable and spent just about every day together. They gave one another space and all out of respect. But would link back together by the end of the night of course. If Angel wasn't in any trouble or wasn't out doing things that she didn't need to do, Tara or Noel pretty much didn't pay them any mind. And the fact that Angel was a junior who didn't run the streets or party and, most importantly, still wasn't pregnant while remaining in a four-year relationship, she was proving a lot of family members wrong despite what they might have said about her.

By her junior year, she had it all figured out, or at least she thought. At eighteen, she and Zion would get married in a small ceremony in Hawaii; they'd have two children, a boy and girl, and Zion would have good jobs, and they'd live in a big house.

Everyone was always asking when they were getting married or when they were going to have a baby. For a long time, Angel didn't think anything of it, but when certain friends and family members would have babies or get engaged, she started to feel a bit pressured which she never felt before. Even though it was something that she longed for, she had a goal to meet and that was to pass the eleventh grade and the twelfth, then maybe after that it might become possible. But all she could do was live in the moment, enjoy being a teenager, and getting through some of the challenges that life threw at her.

School was back in session; Zion was a senior and Angel was a junior. She couldn't believe that all she had was one more year and she could be done. The first few months of school were really good, with her head in the right direction.

But she fell out with one of her very close friends, which was a very nasty fall out and fight. She almost got expelled; it just was a disaster. It got to a point that she fell behind in a few classes because she was bullied, half of the school was against her, so she had to attend school on Saturdays and at different times. Truly thankful for Zion's help for the rides and support because if it wasn't for him, she definitely wouldn't have succeeded. This was not an easy task for Angel, and the two of them would even bump heads at times because she was ready to give up on herself so many times. That was the good thing about the couple; they always encouraged and motivated each other, and when one was down, they lifted each other up.

Also, she knew that she had to set a good example for Legend, Sunshine, and Stormy, so her giving up was out of the question. Though she brought it upon herself, it seemed like Angel always had it hard every school year and would have to play catch to pass at the end of the year. One thing about it, she was going to make it happen regardless of who believed in her or how hard it would be; she was going to get it done and make it happen. Even though she was a junior, there were a few things that she either missed out on or was never introduced to, including drivers training. Everyone in Noel's house took drivers training and got their licenses. Zion actually was the one who taught Angel how to drive and would let her drive from time to time.

Her mother also would give her the car as well, but Noel never would offer or allow it. The school Angel attended still didn't offer any sports, so that was a huge loss for her. At about her age, she should've been applying or at least discussing college and scholarships, but no one sat Angel down or made it a priority to discuss these things; so she had no idea about college or the possibilities it had to offer.

She put in the extra work that was necessary to move forward, and Angel made it a habit to thank the Lord, Himself, and came out on top again. It was anything but easy, and she often thought to herself, "Wow, is this REAL? Did I really make this happen?" She knew she was approaching her last and final year, so she had no choice but to really get herself in check, and go hard. No one made a big deal of her becoming a senior or about purchasing her cap and gown. Angel never really made conversation about it because it would just get ignored anyway.

Going to church was still a thing while living at Noel's, but as Angel got older, she wasn't forced to attend as much as when she was younger. One thing about it, though, if you didn't go to church, you better not be sleeping, and the kitchen and house better be clean when Noel comes home from church, because, if not, you're going to hell with no ice water. Anytime Angel didn't attend church and was home, she made sure things were clean so that she could hide out upstairs when Noel came home, often with a lot of company who came over to eat.

Chapter 18:
GUARDED

Now, talking about church, Angel was saved at a young age – at about nine or ten years old. She always had a big caring heart, very forgiving, and it just came naturally for her. For some reason, she always felt close to God. No, she couldn't speak in tongues, she didn't know what having a relationship with God was about just yet, but she just felt that there was something special about her and that He had a lot to do with it.

Angel became frustrated over time, in part because she didn't understand a lot of things but it was hard to get people to relate. But soon enough, she would have to learn and understand, and a lot of things in life would start to make sense. Everyone has talents and gifts in life; while Angel spent her entire life being brought up and raised in the church, no one ever spoke or prophesied about her life or told her what gifts or talents she had. It was bad enough that she wasn't aware of them herself, so she was even more discouraged and didn't feel special. She used to wonder, "What do I have to do, what do I have to say, what type of lifestyle do I need to live to get your attention, Lord?" She would angrily cry out loud to God. Where was her connection with God? Given what Pyro did to her, she thought that God would take pity on her and make everything better, or at least make all of the bad things go away. Growing up, she knew little about being patient. So, her patience grew thin, and so did her prayers after a while.

That was an odd thing for Angel. Noel was big on church and all but never prayed with her or taught her much about prayer. Tara, on the other hand, didn't go to church and didn't really speak much on praying. Mary didn't attend church but made sure that she would mention to Angel to pray every night. That was one thing about her Auntie Mary; she might've not stepped foot inside of a church, but she watched church service on television at least. Angel didn't understand it then; but as she got older, the more she drifted away from church.

One of Angel's passions was having conversations about church, heaven, hell, angels, demons, life, and death to get people to relate, but a lot of teens her age weren't on her level. They were too busy having sex, trying drugs, drinking, skipping school, and doing a lot of things that they weren't supposed to be doing. Sometimes, when she tried having these conversations, she felt out of place or would wonder if people looked at her weirdly.

Call her lame, but Angel was out of the loop to half of what everyone older was even doing most of the time. She finally got hip when she and about six other schoolmates decided to skip a few classes one day. One person said that their parents were gone at work the entire day, and another person had his girlfriend's car, so why not skip the day right? Usually, Angel never left school, but she allowed them to talk her into leaving that day.

They arrived at the house, and everyone was chilling and talking at first, then suddenly Angel, started seeing weed being passed around and people drinking. She was so caught off guard, she thought to herself, no, this wasn't cool. The dude who drove them there actually liked Angel; he liked her for a long time, but she was in a relationship and didn't like him at that time. They ended up being friends and she would flirt with him a bit. Everyone was smoking and drinking except for Angel; she was the only oddball. Suddenly, everyone noticed and the peer pressure began. Angel never smoked or drank a day in her life nor did it ever cross her mind. But she softened to the peer pressure and wanted to make a good impression in front of the guy who was crushing on her, so she did it.

She grabbed the weed and almost chocked herself to death. Of course, everyone laughed because it was her first time getting high, and she didn't know how to smoke it correctly. Pretty much everyone was coupled up and was chilling; Angel and the guy she liked fooled around a bit, but it got boring so everyone headed back up to the school, which was the dumbest mistake. Everyone went in at the same time, the school had cameras, so the principal saw all of them at once and most of them smelled like marijuana. Angel was as high as a kite, and all she knew was that she wanted to go to the nearest bathroom to wash the smell and high off her face.

She asked God if He could take her high away and promised she would never smoke again. She probably still wouldn't have told Zion about what happened even though they both just would've laughed it off. Angel was just hoping that it wouldn't lead to a phone call home so it wouldn't be such a laughing matter if Noel found out.

But the principal was really cool and down to earth; he gave everybody the choice between three days of suspension or detention. Angel went for detention, and it sucked of course, but at least she could get caught back up in all of her classes, and cool thing was that Noel wouldn't find out anything. Angel tried her hardest to really work and to stay out of trouble being that she wanted and needed to graduate the next year.

And, even more than anything, she had people to piss off who doubted her. There was no denying that Angel had an attitude problem, but she was not always this way. Over the years, she got tired of people taking her kindness for weakness, taking her for granted, or not taking her seriously. She was always finding herself getting hurt all of the time, so she showed people that she had another side to her, and when she did, they didn't like it so much. She got her feelings hurt so much, she had no choice but to put her guard up over the years for protection. Family, friends, associates, it didn't matter who; people in her past made it very hard to get close and to even have a conversation with Angel.

She was very guarded at first, but once she allowed that wall to come down, she could be the most genuine, loving person ever. That was just the problem; no one cared to ask or to know why her guard was up the way it was. Being with Noel had a huge impact on her attitude and her defensiveness her being picked on and having to defend herself time after time, not consciously fitting in with everyone in the house or feeling accepted or purposely being left out of things would leave most people to behave defensively.

So having her guard up was just her mechanism that became a part of who she was. What Angel didn't know was that this bad attitude came from Tara's side. Angel wasn't there just yet, but having an attitude all the time wouldn't get you too far in life, especially when you are content with it as well.

Another reason as to why Angel was guarded in her ways was because most of her life was spent on her own, without someone sitting her down to help her understand certain behaviors and how to correct them. Instead, she was either yelled at, degraded, or spoken to negatively. All those things became a part of who she was after so long. Angel learned to accept a lot of things about who she was, and being guarded was just something that was a part of her. Little did Angel know that it was going to take a lot more than just to have her guard up.

Bad attitude or not, graduation needed to be the main priority. She had a few months left until summer break and as usual, her grades weren't the best. Because of this, she had to put in more effort. Which meant being and staying consistent, staying after school, sometimes, having to arrive before classes started; and if Saturdays were offered, she would volunteer to attend for that day.

Unfortunately, these were the consequences when you don't take school seriously or when you don't try to do your school and homework. Being a teenager and in a long-term relationship, distractions always came along, and there were times that Angel would keep digging holes for herself and continue to fall in them. Until she was ready for change, that would regularly befall her, and Angel could hardly embrace such behavior.

Chapter 19:

THIS THING THEY CALL LIFE

Despite their rocky relationship, Angel finished the rest of her junior year at Tara's, and was there most of the summer as well. The majority of the time she would be with Zion, so she and Tara didn't see much of each other. Every summer was pretty much the same routine as the summer before. Angel never traveled outside of Battle Creek; the furthest Noel ever took everyone to was Chicago.

Angel loved the Chicago trips. Though they would only go to visit other family members and sit around most times, she and a few cousins would walk around the city, which was fun. They shopped there before returning to school, which Angel loved, and Noel would take them to well-known stores; Angel would always have the "flyest" gear.

When she hit seventeen, Noel and Tara pretty much would give her a certain amount of money and would allow for her to do her own shopping. Tara even let her drive a little. Angel would go directly to her destination (often the nail salon) and right back home. Zion would get his hair cut so he allowed Angel to hit a few blocks while she waited for him to get finished. Zion's family had nice cars, and she would always love to show off driving around the hood so everyone could see her. While most teens couldn't wait for their freedom after they graduated, Angel unfortunately did not; she was content going back and forth between homes, but really it was because no one ever talked to her about being independent or having her first apartment. She had no clue about applying for college.

While other teens were busy taking their senior pictures, Noel never brought it to Angel's attention that she needed to do so. She felt left out and unimportant; Angel had no plans about her future. All she knew was to be content with what she had and where she was at in life, not knowing that she had a much better and brighter future ahead. Most of the girls that she grew up with had already graduated before her (they were older), and they all still lived with their parents as well.

Thinking smart, Angel continued to be on birth control, and she made it through high school without becoming pregnant. The summer passed by fast; Angel and her homegirls would attend house parties, and mostly they were packed and off the hook. When Angel would show up with her cousin and homegirls, all eyes were on them, was the best part, of course.

Moving and pushing through the crowds to get through, dudes would always be reaching out to grab on them while passing by. Annoyed at times, Angel couldn't stand to be touched, and don't let it be an ugly dude. Dudes with the audacity to try to touch somebody were a complete turn off. Sometimes, it was good to feel like other people still wanted you, but most of the time Angel sat in front of the yard on the steps, and dudes would ride pass so they could see her. She was really so attractive that not many were bold enough to pull up to talk to her.

Most times, she blew them off – hell, some of them were older men who really made her run in the house. She couldn't stand older men as they made her feel uncomfortable, thanks to Pyro. Angel was psychologically damaged because of what he did to her. She even felt uncomfortable around older uncles and cousins; it pretty much didn't matter who you were, and it made her feel ill at ease, sadly. She hated it that whenever around older males, she always had her guard up. Angel hoped in the future that this would change, so her life wouldn't always be so uncomfortable.

Chapter 20:

THE END OF HER BEGINNING

Angel was so excited going back to school – finally she was a senior – but it still sucked to have to wear the lame uniforms instead of wearing her cute, new clothes to show off. But who cared? All that mattered to her was getting her grades together so that she could be finished with school forever.

It was too bad that her graduating class didn't get the luxuries that other schools were given, but it was cool how some of the younger students looked up to the seniors. Angel tried to be a positive example for them by not doing stuff to get her a detention. Still, she had no driver training, no college applications, not even discussions about preparing for work and getting a job.

The end of Fall was approaching; it was now the end of November, which meant Thanksgiving was near. Though Tara didn't celebrate the holidays, Noel certainly did and that meant Thanksgiving food, which Angel loved. Turkey, ham, dressing, greens, macaroni and cheese, cranberry sauce, chitterlings, and all kind of other foods and desserts. Between Thanksgiving and Christmas was Angel's favorite holiday season, and when it came to cooking soul food, Noel certainly threw down in the kitchen. The holidays came with a bunch of company, with family from out of town adding to the family members who always were around. The house would be packed with people of all different ages.

Sometimes, Angel felt bad for leaving Tara's house to go back to Noel, but it was boring, and she didn't cook on the holidays, so of course Angel would go where her favorite food was cooked. She invited Zion over to hang out with the family, though Zion had a different religion that didn't celebrate the same holidays. She also invited him to church a few times and vice versa.

His church was really quiet, and they would sing songs from a book, while Angel's church was loud, whether it was singing or the pastor preaching. One time, Zion witnessed a few people catching the Holy Ghost, and he nearly wanted to run out of the church because it scared him so much, which gave Angel a good laugh. They learned things from each other and watched each other grow up.

Angel wasn't that excited about Christmas anymore because she learned you're either handed a certain amount of money or you receive nothing at all. No wrapped gifts under the tree. Angel decided to spend Christmas Eve at Tara's house then she would go over to Noel's the following day.

Two days before Christmas Eve, Angel woke up feeling a bit awkward. She told her mother that she had a dream that she never had before. It wasn't a bad dream or anything, but she just felt weird about it. It was about her godfather, Sonny, who lived at the bottom of the apartment house. (The building consisted of four homes, with Tara's apartment at the top.)

Angel was introduced to Sonny, who was old enough to be her granddad, when she was younger. He was respectful, very kindhearted, a great listener, and so on. He always would give Angel and her siblings allowances every week. He even bought them bicycles that would only get stolen from at Noel's house because the uncles would take them to sell them for drugs. But the material things didn't matter to Angel. What she enjoyed were the conversations she and Sonny would have. He was always so patient and understanding; at times, they would sit outside for hours just talking. She was always happy around him and very protective of him.

When she woke up and told Tara about the dream, she had no idea how her life would never be the same after that day. She related how she and Sonny were just sitting in his home and talking in a heartfelt conversation. Tara mentioned that the day before, Sonny had a cold, and they were thinking of taking him to see a doctor.

As they prepared to go downstairs to check and see Sonny, Angel blurted out that Sonny could be dead. Tara looked at her with astonishment, and Angel even questioned herself on why she said it. As they went to knock on the door and on the second knock, Angel started to scream and cry out loud that she knew he was dead. Sonny would never take this long to open or come to the door. Tara continued to knock, but Angel cried out for her to stop knocking. Was it too late? Adding to their stress was the issue of the landlord living an hour away. Finally, Tara and Angel found Sonny deceased, and the police were called.

All Angel could do was cry. She was beyond devastated. She knew that she had to get away, so she hurried and called Zion to come immediately, which he did. He was also saddened by the loss of Sonny; they liked each other a lot. Angel's life would never be the same, especially around Christmas time. She was torn up, and what made it even worse was that Sonny wouldn't be able to attend her graduation – no more talks, no more seeing his great smile or hearing his voice. So sad.

His family didn't have a funeral or gathering for him; they came and took what was valuable from his home. Angel was devastated, and she was more saddened that she didn't collect anything to remember Sonny by. After Christmas break, it was back to school, and Angel was still shaken up by Sonny's death. She didn't know how to cope with it all, especially after seeing his body, which she couldn't get out of her head. She knew that she needed Sonny to be proud of her, so she made it definite that she deserved to walk across that stage in June. By April, Angel moved on with her life of course, but she suffered in silence.

One thing that did excite her was prom. It was her senior prom, and although it was at a different school, it was her time to take Zion. It was her fourth year going to prom, and it was sort of a luxury being a senior. It didn't take Angel long to find the perfect dress either. She found it at the same boutique where she purchased her other prom dresses.

Noel shopped along with her and assured Angel that the dress was appropriate to wear. It was beautiful, in her favorite color of pink, and it shined with dozens of rhinestones, which fascinated her. She had everything all together for prom; she just had to make sure that her attitude and behavior was on point. Her grades were never the best, but she made sure that she was passing. Once again, it was like a roller coaster in school, but she just kept telling herself that it was almost over, so just hang in there.

Because Angel was very independent at a very young age, and she hated having to ask anyone for anything, she got her first job working at McDonald's without anyone telling her to do so. She was excited and very proud of herself, and she only worked weekends because of school. The only thing that might have gotten in her way was transportation.

At last, it was finally time for prom. With all of the chaos finally calming down, she and Zion made it to their last school dance. Heads turned and complimented her on how fabulous her dress was. But upon arrival, Angel and Zion were stopped from entering the hall in which the prom was held. Devastated, she couldn't believe what she was being told. She had purchased their ticket and everything, only to be told that because she was from another school, they refused to let her participate.

Furious, confused, and feeling overwhelmed, Angel refused to give up and tried every option—but none worked out. She asked if she could at least take their prom pictures since they were all dressed up, and the staff allowed it. But with tears, Angel had to walk away from what was supposed to be the greatest time of being a senior.

A month later, the day Angel had been waiting for – graduation – finally arrived. Graduation, the day to walk across the stage. The day started out beyond stressful and crazy. Her outfit that she had custom made was not completed, and she didn't have a backup plan, so she had to think quickly. She was late showing up for the quick rehearsal trying to still get herself together.

At last, it was finally her moment. Tears streamed down her cheeks, reminiscing about all the hard work she put in – all of the trials and tribulations – just for this day to happen. After it was over, she greeted and took pictures with the few family members who did show up. Sadly, Tara didn't show up to support her, but it wasn't the first time that Tara did this. Zion greeted and cheered her on; he was so proud of her. He showed up with her favorite color of pink and white balloons along with dozens of pink roses. This was it, Angel's end to her new beginning, no longer was she a student, no longer was she a child. But as her new life began, little did she know that her life was not to be what she would ever imagine it would be. The world was the opposite of that a life of chaos filled with dark times, as well as times of survival, awaited her.

To Be Continued…

ABOUT THE AUTHOR

Cherrelle Haney, was born in Albion, Michigan, now resides in Battle Creek, where her faith and community have shaped her into the resilient woman she is today. As the eldest of four siblings, she draws strength from her church upbringing.

Cherrelle's life has seen its share of trials, but with determination and faith, she has triumphed. Inspired by her own journey, she shares her story in her books, focusing on overcoming adversity and empowering women. She also volunteers at homeless shelters and advocates for the marginalized.

While Cherrelle has spent over a decade in manufacturing, she's currently pursuing a Bachelor's Degree in Health Administration, driven by a desire to improve healthcare accessibility.

Cherrelle's impact extends beyond her writing, with radio and in-person interviews highlighting her powerful narrative. Her interview on Unfiltered Stories resonated globally, showcasing the influence of her message.

Outside of her professional endeavors, Cherrelle cherishes her role as a mother to her eight-year-old son, Rajah Haney, finding joy in their shared moments. Continuously seeking ways to better her community, she embodies the belief that compassion and shared experiences can overcome life's challenges.

CONTACT THE AUTHOR

If you would like to contact Cherrelle, you can do so at:

Email Address:
angelthechosenone7@gmail.com

Facebook:
https://www.facebook.com/angelthechosenone7

Instagram:
https://www.instagram.com/angelthechosenone7

Printed by Libri Plureos GmbH in Hamburg,
Germany